Managers, Financiers and users

You have decided to take your Excel expertise to the next level. Well done!

Let's see what people who have already learned from the previous edition of the book have to say:

> ☆☆☆☆☆ **Best Intro to VBA you can buy!**
> By Hoomania on January 6, 2016
> This book is laid out with a plan and is written very well.
> It absolutely explained the basics of VBA to me
> and let me try little snippets of code along the way.
>
> I completely recommend it to anyone trying to understand VBA.
> It is short, but I read it slowly and tried out the code as I read about the code.
> I'd suggest everyone do that.
>
> I have purchased other e-books on here and this is easily the best so far for a beginner's level.
> I just have to say thank you to the author who clearly knows her stuff,
> but is focused on TEACHING. Thank you.

This is what Jude Barack said:

> ☆☆☆☆☆ **Great book for beginners - this book does exactly what it promises**
> By Jude Barack on May 13, 2014
> The book takes you one step at a time, each step very clear and following to the next one.
> Just like the title of the book – you don't need to have any knowledge in code writing
> when starting this book – but you can certainly write codes
> when you're done with the book.
> The screen shots are very helpful and clear.
> Recommended for anyone who knows excel and wants to take it to the next level.

And this is what J. Robinson thinks:

> ☆☆☆☆☆ **University text**
> By J. Robison on November 16, 2014
> I use this book in my Introduction to MIS class.
> It's a great way to illustrate programming in a non-technical class.

As you saw, it is not just another book; it is a toolbox that gives you immediate professional priority, even if you are not a programmer.

1

Let me tell you what you can gain from the book:

The book exposes the world of macro commands, creating magic in the field of data processing so that you can:

- Save time
- Keep deadlines
- Streamline work
- Get the appreciation of colleagues and managers

So what are you going to learn?

- Right after reading the "Macro Recording" chapter, you will save many hours of work by learning how to record an absolute macro and relative macro (yes, there are several kinds of macro recordings). The macro recording will help you when you want to learn new commands in the future and when you are not familiar with their syntax.
- Right after the "Cells and Ranges" chapter, all your work will reach another level when you become an expert and gain the ability to access objects in a file in order to refer to cells, columns, and rows. Write in them, copy them, and color them so that they stand out.
- On the "Variables" and "Conditions" chapters, you will become more precise in data processing. Using the results obtained, you can make sophisticated executive decisions (and as you know, knowledge is power) after learning how to create flexible macro commands that meet various needs.
- You will save more time by using the "Loops" chapter as you elegantly create loops that shorten long, tiresome, and repeating processes, which is another significant advantage that can be performed only in VBA.
- Your colleagues will feel comfortable working with you after you learn how to get data from them and present them with

messages in a friendly and accessible manner in the "Interaction with the User" chapter, and you will feel like a real pro!

- All the work you've learned to do so far will turn into a complete, comprehensive, and packed product when you use the tools you learn on the new "Files" and "Folders" chapters.

See what another user wrote about the benefits and the pleasure he derives from the use of the book:

I am looking forward to hearing from you regarding how the book was useful to you, too!

Ma'ayan Poleg

Abstract

Microsoft Excel has, over the years, become the greatest software in the field of electronic worksheets.

Its strength is that it meets the demands of huge numbers of users worldwide. Nonetheless, despite the advancement and expanding use of this software, there is ever-increasing demand from the end users, much of which can only be solved by VBA programming (Visual Basic for Applications).

Therefore, "Excel VBA – In Everyday Language" has been written in order to provide a response to the growing demand for the advanced capabilities of Microsoft Excel.

This book was written:

- For the "non-programmers" among us who have to create the same reports in Microsoft Excel time and again, and would like to automate the process.
- For people who wish to develop forms, screens and applications for data management within their organization.
- For individuals who wish to turn Microsoft Excel into a powerful tool in their daily work.

During the writing process, I tried to visualize Microsoft Excel software and the VB editor through the eyes of the end users: people who may not have programming background, but aspire to reap the utmost from the program.

For this reason the book, which is based on many years of experience in programming and training, has been written in everyday language, using as few technical terms as possible, to make it easy to read.

My objective, while writing this book, was to convey the basic and commonly used principles of VBA language and allow beginners, taking their first steps, to learn without requiring any personal training.

For this purpose, there are attached files of exercises accompanying the book. These can be downloaded from bit.ly/Excel-VBA.

The exercise files are in .xls format, allowing the end users to use either the "Ribbon" Versions (2007 and higher) or other older versions of Microsoft Excel.

This new edition has undergone extensive processing and addresses Microsoft Excel 2013 users, along with explanations for anyone using previous ribbon versions. Therefore, wherever there is a significant difference between Excel 2013 and the previous versions, explanations have been provided in full.

I wish you a pleasant entry into the world of VBA!

Maayan Poleg

Table of Contents

Disclaimer

This book was written for Microsoft Excel users who want to expand their knowledge of this software.

Considerable effort has been invested to write a book that is as complete and reliable as possible, although that does not imply any guarantee.

The author is not responsible for any loss or damage which may be caused to any individual or organization, due to the information contained in this book.

It is highly recommended to back-up all work data prior to executing any changes.

Introduction

VBA (Visual Basic for Applications) is a programming language designed for use with a variety of Microsoft Office software. It allows you to dramatically expand the basic options inherent in the software with the creation of tailor-made, customized applications. This book focuses on the VBA language for Microsoft Excel.

Why should you become familiar with VBA language?

There are two main reasons:

Firstly, it makes it possible to utilize a macro to automate frequently repeated processes.

Secondly, the VBA programming language enables the user to add features that are not directly supported by Microsoft Excel, such as:

- Providing user alerts and notifications
- Receiving data from the user
- Performing loops on data
- Creating forms
- And much more...

By writing VBA codes you can enrich Microsoft Excel files, turning them into powerful tools for your personal needs, or the needs of your organization.

Reading Guidelines

Here is a short guide to the terminology used in this book:

- When the names of two keys appear with the sign "+" between them, you should press on both the keys simultaneously.

  For example, to open the VB editor, you must press on the

15

keyboard shortcut Alt+F11 (in other words, hold down the Alt key when pressing F11).

- Tips, comments and programming code snippets will appear in grey boxes.

For example:

```
Sub FontSize()
        ActiveCell.Font.Size = 14
End Sub
```

- Practical exercises will appear in a numbered list.

For example:

```
1. Open the VB editor
2. Add a module
```

- The sub-menu selection from the Main Menu will appear with the sign "→" to indicate the order of operations.

For example:

```
Select 'Developer' tab → 'Record Macro'
```

- Although there is no need to add blank lines between the different parts of the code, they were added to make reading easier, and to clarify matters for beginners.

Basic Terms

This chapter contains a list of basic terms.

These terms will be clarified during the learning process and practice.

VBA	An event-oriented language that relates to objects.
Macro/Code	A Sequence of actions that enables process automation (macros can be recorded or manually written).
Objects	The "Building Blocks" of the program: workbook, worksheet, range, column, row etc., You can perform various actions on objects such as calculation, design, copying, etc.
Collections	Grouping objects of the same type, for example – a collection of worksheets or charts.
Object Properties	Each object has properties. Background, for example, is a property of a range.

Method	Actions on objects, for example, you can run the method (action) 'copy' on a range-type object.
Event	Each action that takes place on a worksheet, or a workbook such as - clicking, selecting, opening etc.
Module	A component of the VB editor which can store code lines in it.
Absolute Macro	A Macro that operates on a pre-set range, regardless of the current location in the worksheet.
Relative Macro	A Macro that operates on ranges in accordance with the current location in the worksheet.
Routine	A Sequence of actions to perform.
Variable	Memory "stack" designed to store temporary values while the code is running.

Developer Tab

Starting from the Microsoft Excel 2007 version, the user interface has changed significantly, and now displays "ribbons" instead of toolbars.

Therefore, Excel 2007 and higher are called the "ribbon" versions.

In these versions, the different actions related to macro and code writing appear in the "Developer" tab.

The tab does not appear as a default, and must be added manually.

Adding the Developer Tab to Microsoft Excel 2010-2016 version

1. Click the **FILE** tab.

2. Click **Options**

3. Click Customize Ribbon

4. Select Developer, as shown in the following image:

5. Click OK

6. The Developer tab will appear:

Adding the Developer Tab to Microsoft Excel 2007 version

1. Click to open the menu.
2. Click Excel Options
3. Under Popular, select **'Show Developer tab in the Ribbon'**:

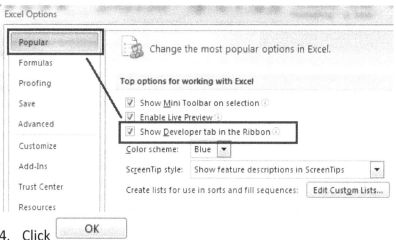

4. Click OK
5. The Developer tab will appear:

Security

Security Level

Using macros can optimize processes and improve work. However, if not used carefully, they can cause lots of damage. For example, a macro can delete all the files in a folder.

Therefore, Microsoft has made the macros unavailable by default. However, it does allow the user to change their own security level according to their needs.

Please note, in order to allow the running of macros you'll have to downgrade the security level.

Macro Security Settings

1. On the **Developer** tab, in the **Code** group, click

   ⚠ Macro Security

2. The following window will open:

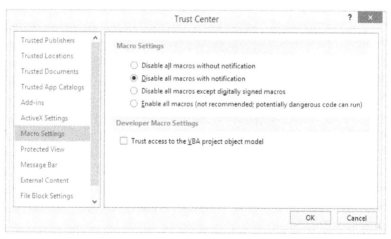

3. Select the desired security level.

Trust Center

Microsoft Office 2007 was the first version to introduce the 'Trust Center', where you can change the security settings of Office files.

Trusted Locations

Trusted Location is a folder that enables the files saved in it to be opened without being checked by the Trust Center's security features.

Make sure to save only files from a reliable origin in this folder.

Trusted Locations Settings

In Excel 2010-2016

1. Click **FILE** to open the menu.

2. Click **Options**

In Excel 2007

1. Click 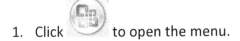 to open the menu.

2. Click 📑 Excel Options

Adding the Trusted Locations

3. Under **Trust Center**, click **Trust Center Settings**, as shown in the following image:

4. The following window will open:

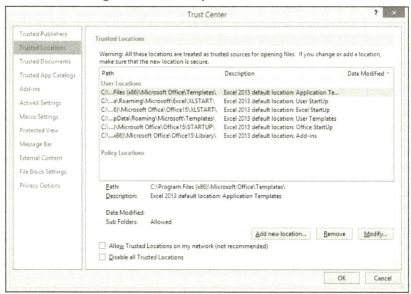

5. Click Add new location.

6. The following window will open:

```
┌────────────────────────────────────────────────────────────────┐
│          Microsoft Office Trusted Location      ?    [ × ]       │
├────────────────────────────────────────────────────────────────┤
│  Warning: This location will be treated as a trusted source for  │
│  opening files. If you change or add a location, make sure that  │
│  the new location is secure.                                     │
│  Path:                                                           │
│  ┌────────────────────────────────────────────────────────────┐ │
│  │                                                            │ │
│  └────────────────────────────────────────────────────────────┘ │
│                                               ┌──────────────┐   │
│                                               │   Browse...   │   │
│                                               └──────────────┘   │
│  ☐ Subfolders of this location are also trusted                  │
│  Description:                                                    │
│  ┌────────────────────────────────────────────────────────────┐ │
│  │                                                            │ │
│  └────────────────────────────────────────────────────────────┘ │
│  Date and Time Created:   16/05/2015 14:33 PM                    │
│                            ┌──────────┐   ┌──────────┐           │
│                            │    OK    │   │  Cancel  │           │
│                            └──────────┘   └──────────┘           │
└────────────────────────────────────────────────────────────────┘
```

7. Click Browse to select the desired folder, and then click
   OK .

   You can set the subfolder in the location to also be considered as 'trusted'.

8. The folder will be added to the trusted locations list.

Files with macro commands in the folder will be activated without notification.

Removing a Trusted Location

In the Trusted Locations window, as shown in section 4 above, select the location you wish to remove from the trusted locations list and click Remove

Saving Files

Until the Microsoft Excel 2003 version, files were saved with an "xls" extension.

In the "Ribbon" versions, the extension of the Excel workbook was changed to "xlsx".

xlsx files **cannot** store Macro commands.

In order to enable the workbook to save the macros, it should be saved with the "xlsm" extension.

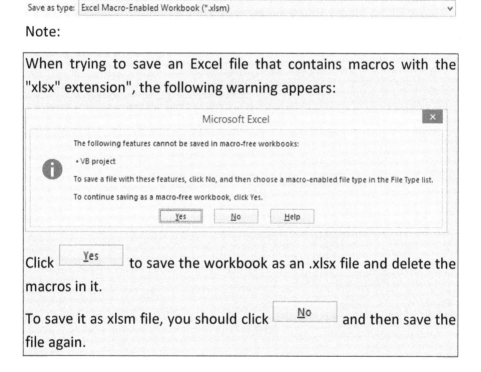

Note:

When trying to save an Excel file that contains macros with the "xlsx" extension", the following warning appears:

Click [Yes] to save the workbook as an .xlsx file and delete the macros in it.

To save it as xlsm file, you should click [No] and then save the file again.

Important to Know:

Saving the file with the .xls extension will allow you to run macros in the Ribbon versions as well, but it will limit the number of rows and columns in the workbook, in accordance with their number in Excel 2003.

(In the Excel 2003 version the number of rows is 65,536, whereas in the ribbon versions the number of rows is 1,048,576).

Visual Basic Editor (VBE)

Enter VB Editor

On the Developer tab, click [Macros]

Or, click the shortcut key **Alt+F11**.

VB Editor

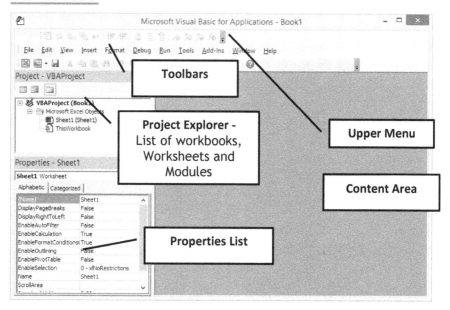

Please note that, by default, the VB editor opens without modules.

Add a module by selecting **Insert → Module** (you cannot write in the gray content area if the module has not been added).

The module will be added to the list in the Project window.

Note:

The VB editor might open differently on your computer. Later in this chapter, you will learn how to adjust the display of the window so that it appears similar to the example.

The Structure of the VB Editor

The VB editor window is divided into several areas:

- Menu – contains menus such as File, Edit, etc.

- Toolbar – contains the most useful commands from the menus.

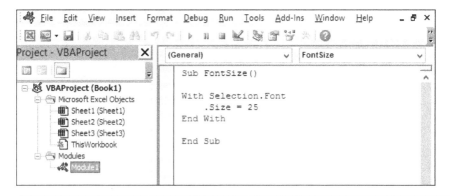

- Content Area – here you can write, edit and run the codes. Most activities in the content area will be done in Modules.
- Explorer - Displays the list of projects, workbooks, worksheets and modules. If the window does not appear, click **View →Project Explorer**, or press the shortcut key **Ctrl+R**.
- To display the codes, double-click on the desired workbook, worksheet or module in the explorer window.

- If you have opened a number of workbooks, note which workbook you are writing the code in, because this is the workbook the macro will be saved in (you can check that you are actually writing in the correct workbook using Project Explorer).
- There is no significance to the module in which the codes are written, as long as they are written in the correct workbook.

- Every time you open Microsoft Excel and record a macro, it is recorded in a new module.
- As long as the file is open, all codes are recorded in the same module.
- The location of the recorded macro cannot be controlled, but you can move the codes from one module to another after recording by using "cut and paste".

Adapting the VB Editor Workspace

To change the VB editor workspace, press **Tools → Options**.

Editor Tab

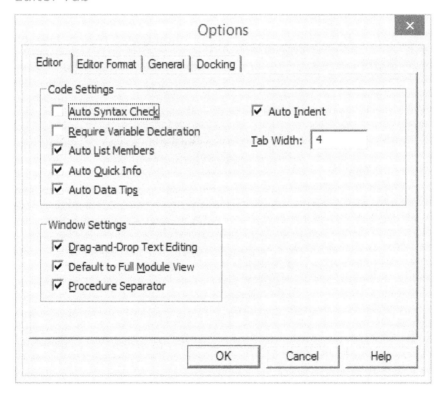

Auto Syntax Check	Determines whether an alert will appear whenever a syntax error is detected.
Require Variable Declaration	Requires the user to declare variables comprehensively. Note - If you want to make the user declare variables in a specific module only, you can use the Option Explicit command at the top of the module (details of the 'declaration of variables' on page 65).
Auto List Members	Offers help when typing the command by showing the list of properties belonging to it (see page 65).
Auto Quick Info	Displays the required arguments while typing a command.
Auto Data Tips	When you place the cursor on it, it displays the variable value while the macro is running in a step by step mode.

Editor Format Tab

This allows you to set the font formats (type and size) for the codes, comments, breakpoints, etc.:

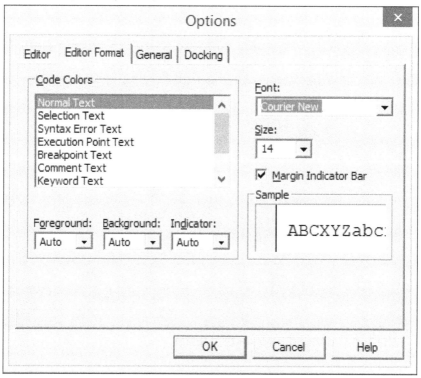

In order to select the design, highlight the desired option.

Normal Text changes the text color used for writing code.

Selection Text is used to change the selected text color.

Execution Point Text is used to change the color of the next line executed.

Note:

You can see the settings preview in the sample window.

General Tab

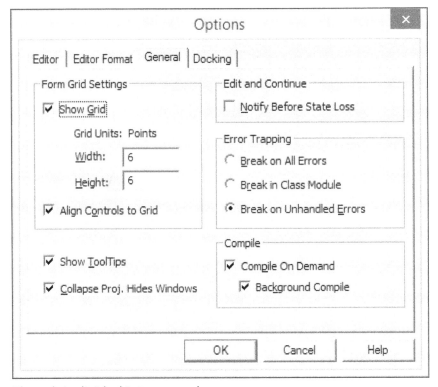

The tab is divided into several areas:

Form Grid Settings	Refers to the grid lines when designing forms.
Edit and Continue	Allows you to determine whether a warning message will be displayed; warning that specific actions will reset variables
Error Trapping	Allows a choice between different options to stop running the code when an error occurs.

Docking Tab

This allows you to determine which of the windows will be fixed to the screen and which will "float".
When a window is fixed to the screen you can attach it to one side of the editor (usually the bottom or side of the window):

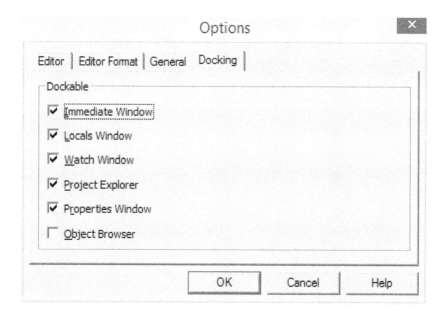

A Moment Before We Start...

Code writing can be simple, if you follow a few basic rules.

It is not random, that a VBA file is called a "Project"; it is absolutely a project and, as with every project, proper planning and adhering to rules will allow for smooth and efficient implementation later on. Or, as the wise men said: "Think before you act".

So, before sitting down to record a macro or write a code, read the following instructions:

- Create a backup copy: Before you start writing a code, create a backup copy of the original workbook so you can recover data if necessary.
- Definition of project goals: Ahead of time, define the purpose of the code and the desired final product. Such a definition will enable you to evaluate the development time required, as well as the necessary resources for implementation.
- Decomposition of a project into its components: Which tasks in the code must be developed in order to produce the final, pre-defined product?
- Writing the code: This is the practical part of writing a macro (VBA code). The main contents of this book focus on "How to write what you need".
- Leave time for testing: Allow yourself the right to be wrong. There was never a programmer who wrote a code that worked perfectly the first time. After you finish reading this book, you will not be exempted from testing. Be prepared for something in the code not working the first time. That's to be expected, because it happens to everyone ...

- Write Comments: There is nothing more annoying than going back to a code you wrote a year ago and trying to figure it out...
- Don't know how to write? Record! Many times, you will discover that you don't know how to write a specific code command. I advise you to record it. Then view the code and learn the relevant commands.
- There is nothing like F1: Get into the habit of using the VBA help. Often you will discover that the nuances of the commands can change their outcome. Placing the cursor on a command and pressing F1 on the keyboard will display relevant explanations for that command, as well as options and further examples.
- Do not re-invent the wheel: Check the Internet, do research, consult forums and ask questions. Efficient searching can save you many hours of work that someone else has already done!

Objects

The way in which the VB Editor communicates with Microsoft Excel is by referring to objects.

Examples of objects are: the application itself (Microsoft Excel software), a workbook, a worksheet, a row, a column, a chart and so on.

The objects have:

- **Properties** – for example, size is a property of the object 'Font'.
- **Methods** – for example, copying is a method (action) that can be performed on a 'Range' object.
- **Events** – for example, selecting a cell or changing a value are events that can activate a macro.
- **Related Objects** – for example, there are objects related to the worksheet objects, such as rows, columns, etc.

The objects are arranged hierarchically, with the main object being the Microsoft Excel software itself, which enables actions at the software level. Reference is made to it using the Application command.

Note:

The explanations for writing commands will appear in the chapter **'Writing Macro Commands in VB editor'** on page 61.

Referring to cells and objects will be covered in the **'Cells** and Ranges' chapter on page 71.

Please note that in some cases you can omit the name of the "parent object", for example, the command to add a worksheet is:

Application.Worksheets.Add

This can also be written in an abbreviated form:

```
Worksheets.Add
```

But, the command:

```
Range("A1").Name = "FirstCell"
```

Is significantly different from the command:

```
Worksheets("Sheet1").Range("A1").Name = "FirstCell"
```

This is due to the fact that the first code applies the name "FirstCell" to cell A1 in the active worksheet, while the second code applies the name "FirstCell" to cell A1 in "Sheet 1", regardless of the worksheet from which we run the code.

Macro Recording

The basic way to automate processes is by recording a macro directly from the Microsoft Excel software.

Display 'Record Macro' Window

Click on  Record Macro in the Developer tab.
The following window will open:

In this window you will be asked to name the macro (it is recommended to change the default name provided by the program into a significant name that describes the code operation).

Rules for the Macro Names:

- The macro name must begin with a letter (not a number or other sign).
- Spaces are not allowed in a macro name (in other words, the macro should have a one-word name).

- You may use the underscore as a separator between two words, i.e. Sum_Range.
- Do not choose Microsoft Excel's reserved names like "print" or "save". To avoid problems that might arise due to reserved names, you can add the prefix "My", i.e. My_Print to each macro.
- It is recommended to assign a name that accurately describes the meaning of the macro.

Note:
An error message will appear if you give a macro an illegal name.

In the next step you will have to choose where to store (save) the macro:

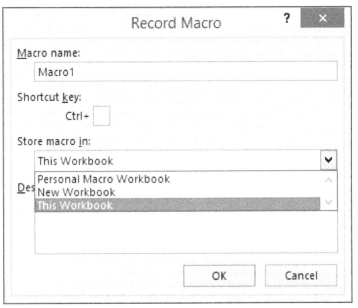

Personal Macro Workbook – the macro will be recorded automatically into the "Personal.xlsb" file, which is loaded when Excel starts, and is available for all workbooks.

This Workbook – the macro will be recorded in the current workbook, and will only be available when this file is open.

New Workbook – the macro will be recorded in the new workbook.

You can choose a shortcut key to run the macro.

Please note, there are many shortcut keys in Microsoft Excel software. For example, Ctrl+S is used for saving, Ctrl+P is used for printing, etc.

While assigning a shortcut, the combination you choose will replace the shortcut key action in the workbook where the code was saved. Therefore, it's preferable to use shortcuts that are used infrequently.

You can also add the "Shift" key by holding it down and simultaneously pressing the desired key (there is no need to press the "Ctrl" key, which appears by default).

To confirm, click OK

The macro is now recorded and the button Record Macro will be replaced by the Stop Recording button.

Another important button is the Use Relative References button. This determines whether the macro you record will run as an "absolute reference" (which means it will run on the range of cells that were selected while the macro was recorded, regardless of your current position in the worksheet); or as a "relative reference" (which means, relative to your position in the worksheet).

Relative Recording Exercise:

1. Open a new workbook.
2. Select cell A1.
3. Select a new macro recording.
4. Give it the name 'YellowHello'.
5. Store it in 'This workbook'.
6. Assign it the shortcut Ctrl+q:

7. Click ‾‾‾‾OK‾‾‾‾
8. Click the Relative Reference button ⬚ (this way the macro will run on any cell selected. Otherwise, the macro will

always work on the range of cells selected when recording, regardless of the cursor position when running the macro).

9. Paint the cell background in yellow

10. Write "Hello".

11. Press Enter on the keyboard.

12. Click the Stop Recording button ■

13. Now select any cell in the worksheet and run the macro using the key combination Ctrl+q.

14. Save the workbook with the name 'Macro Recording'.

Absolute Recording Exercise

1. Open the file 'Macro Recording'.

2. Select a new macro recording.

3. Give the macro the name 'GreenHello'.

4. Store it in 'This Workbook'.

5. Assign it the shortcut Ctrl+m:

6. Click OK

7. If the Relative Reference button is active, deactivate it by clicking it again.

8. Select cell A1.

9. Press Enter on the keyboard.

10. Paint the cell background in green

11. Write "Hello".

12. Press Enter on the keyboard.

13. Click the Stop Recording button

14. Delete the content and format of cell A2 (you can find this option under the Home tab → Edit category).

15. Select any cell in the worksheet and run the macro with the Ctrl+m combination.

Running a Macro

There are several ways to run the macro you have just recorded.

Note:

If you are unable to run the macro due to a security level issue, follow the instructions on page 21.

Running a macro from the Developer tab

1. On the Developer tab, click Macros
2. A list with all recorded macros will appear.
3. Select the macro (you will recognise the name you assigned to it when it was recorded).
4. Click Run.

Running a macro using a shortcut key

1. Select any cell in the worksheet.
2. Press on the pre-determined key combination.

Running a Macro by Assigning a Button from the Form Controls

Insert

1. On the Developer tab, click

2. Select a button:

3. Draw a virtual square in the worksheet.
4. The Assign Macros dialog box will appear.
5. Select the desired macro.
6. Click [OK]
7. Click the button to run the macro.

Editing the Button

To edit the button, make sure it is framed (if you click on it while it is unframed, the macro associated with it will start running. To select it, if it is not framed, right-click on it).

A right-click will display the associated menu where you can edit the text, assign a different macro, etc.

Running a macro by adding a button to the Quick Access toolbar

1. Click the drop-down arrow in the quick access toolbar and select More Commands:

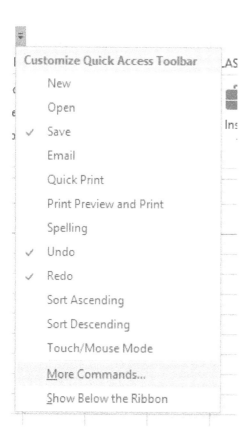

2. In the Choose commands from list, select Macros:

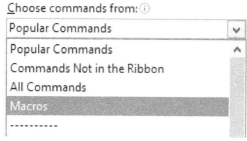

3. Select the desired macro.

4. Click Add.

5. Click [OK]

6. The button will appear on the quick access toolbar:

Customizing the Ribbon (only for the 2010-2016 versions)

Excel 2010/2013 allows you to create new tabs and add macro commands into custom groups in existing tabs.

Creating a new tab:

1. Click the **FILE** tab.

2. Click **Options**

3. From the categories list, select **Customize Ribbon**

4. Click **New Tab**

5. The new tab will be added to the ribbon tabs:

6. You can rename the tab by clicking [Rename...]

Adding a New Group (in a new tab or in an existing tab):

1. Click the [FILE] tab.

2. Click [Options]

3. From the categories list, select [Customize Ribbon]

4. Select the tab that you want to add a group to.

5. Click [New Group]

6. A new group will be created in the tab you have selected:

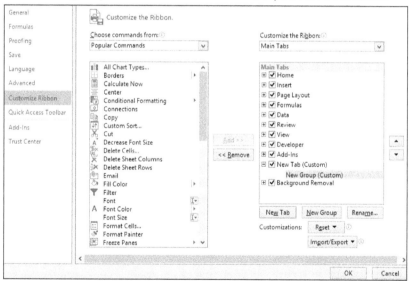

7. You can rename the group by clicking [Rename...]

Adding a macro to the group:

1. Click FILE
2. Click Options
3. From the categories list select Customize Ribbon
4. Click Macros.
5. Select the desired macro from the list.
6. Select the group that you want to add the macro to and click Add >>
7. The button will be added to the group you have selected.

Using Macro Recording for Process Efficiency

Often during our work, we deal with repetitive tasks.

Instead of performing them over and over again, we can record a macro to perform them automatically, with a single click!

For example, if we own a store and need to update the inventory periodically, we can build a table in a fixed structure:

	A	B	C	D
1	Inventory			
2	Product	Price	Qty	Total
3	Computer	550	55	30250
4	Monitor	715	85	60775
5	Keyboard	35	40	1400
6	Mouse	15	60	900

And format it as follows:

	A	B	C	D
1	Inventory			
2	Product	Price	Qty	Total
3	Computer	550	55	30250
4	Monitor	715	85	60775
5	Keyboard	35	40	1400
6	Mouse	15	60	900

To make it more efficient, we can record a macro that will perform the following actions:

1. Center the title.

2. Change the title font size to 14.

3. Add borders to the table.

4. Color the titles.

From now on, instead of performing four separate actions each time we want to design the data table, we can do it with a single click!

The macro recording:

1. Open the workbook "**Inventory.xls**" in the worksheet '**January**'.
2. Open the '**macro recording**' window (see instructions on page 39).
3. Name the macro "**Inventory**" and store it in **this workbook** (you can assign a shortcut key to run it).
4. Make sure that the **Relative Reference** button is deactivated.
5. Select the range A1:D1 and click the **Merge and Center** button.
6. Change the font size to 14.
7. Select the range A1:D6 and add a border to it ⊞
8. Select the range A2:D2 and add a background to it.
9. Select the range A3:A6 and add a background to it.
10. Click the "**Stop Recording**" button.
11. Select the worksheet '**February**' and run the macro.

Watching the recorded macro from the VB Editor and improving it

Watching the Code

Watching a recorded code is a fundamental and easy way to learn how to write macro commands.

As you have already learned in the chapter "**Running a Macro**" on page 45, there are several ways to run a macro.

An additional method is to run the macro directly from the VB editor (make sure that there are macro commands in the editor first).

Running a macro

1. Open the workbook "**Inventory.xls**".
2. Select the worksheet '**March**'.
3. Click
4. Make sure that the macro Inventory is selected.
5. Click Edit.
6. Now you can see all the previously recorded commands translated to VBA code.
7. To run the macro click the Run button in the toolbar. Or, select **Run → Run Sub**.

Or, press the **F5** key on the keyboard:

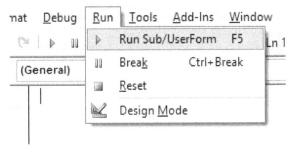

Running the macro step-by-step

Sometimes you need to run the macro step-by-step (which means, one line after another) to test it.

1. Open the workbook "**Cell Selection.xls**".
2. Select the worksheet '**Selection**'.
3. Click
4. Make sure the macro SelectCells is selected.
5. Click Edit.
6. Press the **F8** key on the keyboard.

```
Sub Selection()
        Range("a1").Select
        Range("a2").Select
        Range("a3").Select
        Range("a4").Select
        Range("a5").Select
End Sub
```

Please note, the highlighted line (in the VB editor it will be marked in yellow), is the next line to be executed.

In the example above, cell A1 is already selected, and the next time you press on the F8 key, cell A2 will be selected and so on.

Stopping a macro from running

You can stop the action of the macro while it is running in a state of '**step-by-step**' with the Stop button in the toolbar.

Sometimes it may be necessary to stop a macro from running, despite the fact that it started by order of the **F5** key or some other code. For example, a macro that continues to run because it has entered an infinite loop. The way to stop it is by pressing the **Esc** key or the shortcut key **Ctrl+Break**.

Set a breakpoint

You can run a macro automatically up to a specific point, and then run it manually, to check the code snippet after the breakpoint (for example, a macro that runs a loop on 1000 rows in a worksheet, and then makes some calculations. Adding a breakpoint after the loop will save you from having to run the loop code manually 1000 times, but will allow you to check the calculations that follow it).

The VB editor allows you to insert a breakpoint by clicking on the left gray border of the editor (or by pressing **F9** while the cursor is placed at some point on the relevant code line).

You can add a breakpoint in a code line that contains any action, or in the macro name (you cannot add breakpoints in code lines that contain comments or declarations about variables):

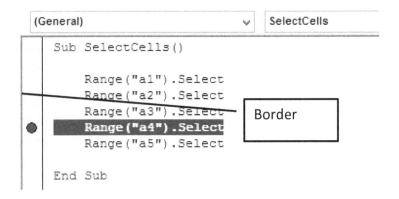

```
(General)                              ∨    SelectCells

    Sub SelectCells()

        Range("a1").Select
        Range("a2").Select
        Range("a3").Select          Border
        Range("a4").Select
        Range("a5").Select

    End Sub
```

The line will be highlighted in red, and a dark red dot will appear next to it.

Now, you can press the F5 key to run the code that will stop when it reaches the breakpoint. From there, you can run it manually, step-by-step, by pressing **F8**, or run it to the end using the **F5** key.

In the example above, pressing on **F5** will run the code automatically for the first 3 lines (it will select cell A1, then cell A2, then cell A3, where it will stop).

Now you can continue running it manually by pressing **F8**, which will select cell A4, or by pressing **F5**, which will make it run to the end.

To remove the breakpoint, press on the dark red dot again.

Exercise – breakpoint:
1. Open the workbook "**Cell Selection.xls**".
2. Select the worksheet '**Selection**'.

3. Click  Macros
4. Make sure the macro SelectCells is selected.

56

5. Click Edit.

6. Add a breakpoint next to the 4th code line (which selects cell A4).

7. Press **F5** on the keyboard.

8. In the "**Selection**" worksheet, check which cell the cursor is located in.

9. Continue running the code step-by-step by pressing **F8**.

Tip:

To view the changes that are being made to the file while the program is running, minimize the VB editor window in a way that will not hide the workbook, and then run it.

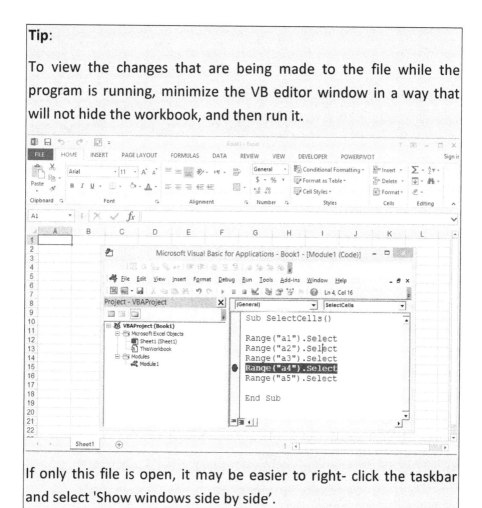

If only this file is open, it may be easier to right- click the taskbar and select 'Show windows side by side'.

Code Improvement

When a macro is recorded, all of the properties of the object are also recorded, even those which were not changed.

For example, let's record a macro which changes the font size to 14. The macro recording will produce the following code:

```
Sub FontSize()
 With Selection.Font
        .Name = "Arial"
        .Size = 14
        .Strikethrough = False
        .Superscript = False
        .Subscript = False
        .OutlineFont = False
        .Shadow = False
        .Underline = xlUnderlineStyleNone
        .ThemeColor = xlThemeColorLight1
        .TintAndShade = 0
        .ThemeFont = xlThemeFontMinor
 End With
```

While checking the code we see many code lines with properties not chosen by us (i.e. the font name, an underline etc.).

Multiple lines slow the action of the macro, and make the code less distinct. This could make the code difficult to revise at a later stage. Examining the code shows that all the features appearing in the **Font** tab, under the **Format Cells** option, were recorded:

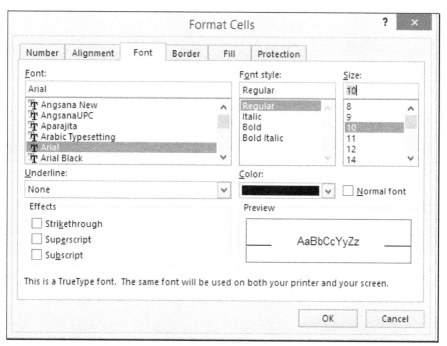

We can change the recorded code, and delete all of those unnecessary properties, by selecting the lines and pressing the Delete key.

Even if we are not yet familiar with VBA, we can understand from the code itself which lines to delete and which to keep.

In the above example, the only property we changed is the font size, so all the other attributes (such as font name, strikethrough, superscript, etc.) are unnecessary. The shorter code will look like this:

```
Sub FontSize()
  With Selection.Font
      .Size = 14
  End With
End Sub
```

Exercise - Improving the recorded code:

1. Open a new workbook.
2. Write in cell A1 the word "Hello".
3. Click Record Macro
4. Name it Improve and Press OK.
5. Change the font type.
6. Click Stop Recording

7. Click Macros
8. Make sure that the macro Improve is selected.
9. Click Edit.
10. Watch the code.
11. Delete all unnecessary code lines.
12. Run the revised code and check whether it performs as required.

Writing Macro Commands in VB editor

After learning about the structure of the VB editor, how to record macros, and even how to improve them, it's time to "get your hands dirty" and start writing your own codes.

Most of the macro commands will be written on two main levels:

1. Module level macro – this macro will be available on all worksheets of the workbook.

2. Sheet level macro – this macro will be available on the specific worksheet on which it was written (to make it work on other worksheets too, you must clearly specify it in the commands themselves).

The structure of macro commands

A VBA macro command is called a **Routine**.

The routine starts with the word Sub, followed by the macro name. Each routine ends with: End Sub.

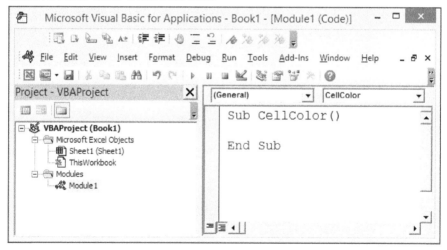

In the example above we notified the VB editor that we are about to write a macro named "CellColor".

61

Please note, as soon as you type the word "**Sub**" and the name of the macro, and press Enter, the command End Sub automatically appears, as well as the brackets after the macro name.

Code Writing Conventions

In order to make the code clear, there are a few writing conventions:

Comments – free text that describes the code.

To add a comment into the VBA code, type an apostrophe (') before the comment. The compiler will ignore what is written after the apostrophe, but the comments will help us to understand what we wrote, if we open the file at some future date (adding a comment can save hours of work trying to understand "what the poet meant" when he wrote the code ...).

The comment lines are automatically highlighted in green, to easily distinguish between them and the other lines of code.

A comment can be typed anywhere on the line (even next to the code line itself).

' This Macro colors the active cell
ActiveCell.Interior.Color = vbGreen

Tip:
Before deleting a code line, it is recommended to mark it as a comment and check whether or not the code runs well without it.
This way, if we see that the code line is important (despite having thought it was unnecessary), we will not have to retype it, but merely delete the apostrophe (').

Use text indentation – pressing TAB on the keyboard causes text indentation of the line and allows us to see the code structure more clearly. The text indentation does not affect the code itself.

It is customary to use text indentation for IF commands (page 107), With commands (page 91) and while using loops (page 111).

Split lines – it is customary to split long lines by adding a space and then an underscore, as shown in the following example:

The command that colors the interior of cell A1 in yellow

```
Range("a1").Interior.Color = vbYellow
```

can be split into two lines:

```
Range("a1").Interior.Color = _
vbYellow
```

The VB editor refers to the two lines as one continuous line. Note the space before the underscore!

Syntax

In order to write VBA codes, we must become familiar with the structure of the commands.

The command structure is, firstly, "**on what**". In other words, what is the object we are referring to? Only then comes the "**what**", meaning, what is the action (property or method) that we want to perform?

For example:

```
Range("a1").Copy
```

According to the explanation above:

"On what?" – on cell A1

"What? " – copy

This means that in VBA language we write the sentence as follows: "On cell A1 perform an action of copy".

The two parts of the command are separated by a dot (.).
Another example:

```
Range("a1").Interior.Color = vbRed
```

"On what?" - on the interior of cell A1

"What?" – color the cell in red

Tip:

The VB editor allows auto-completion:

Start typing the object name and press the shortcut key **Ctrl+Spacebar**. If this is the only object starting with those letters, it will be completed automatically. If there are other objects, a list will appear, from which you can select the desired object by double-clicking it or by pressing the tab key, as illustrated in the following figure:

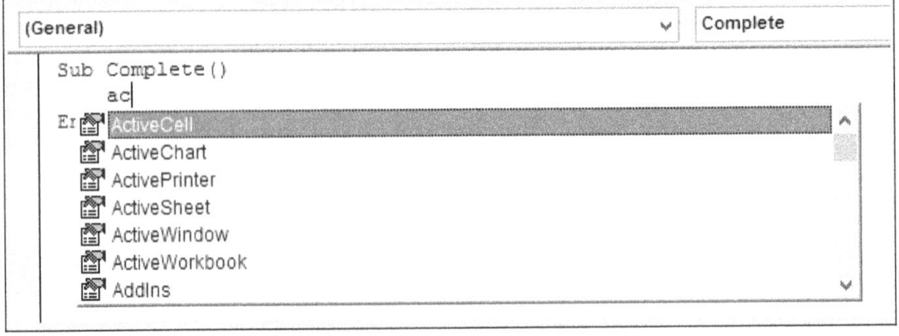

In the same way, you will know which methods and properties exist for each object. Press the shortcut key **Ctrl+Spacebar** after the dot which separates the object from its methods and properties, as illustrated in the following figure:

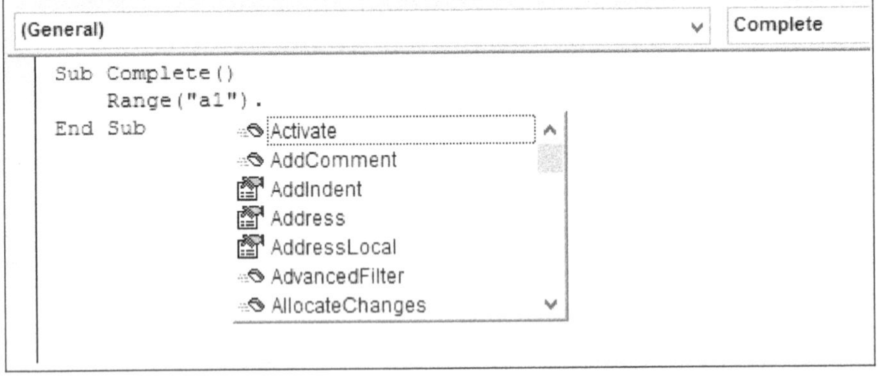

Recommendation:

Write the code in lowercase letters only.

If the code is correct, the compiler will automatically change the first letters of each command into uppercase letters when you move to the next line.

This way you can check if the syntax is written correctly.

66

If the commands, or some of them, remain in lowercase letters, there is an error in the syntax or the spelling.

Declaration on Variables and Objects

This will be done by the Dim command in the structure:

Dim x As Y

Dim MyName As String
Dim MyChart As Chart

For more details about the declaration, see page 87.

Applying a value to a variable

This is done by the symbol "="

Dim MyName As String
MyName = "Jenny Moore"

You can apply values that appear in Microsoft Office settings to a variable:

Dim MyName As String
MyName = Application.UserName

In the above example we entered the username that was set when installing the Microsoft Office package into the variable MyName, using the command **Application.UserName**

Applying an object to a variable

This can be done using the **SET** command followed by an equals (=) sign.

In the following example, we insert the object **Application.WorksheetFunction**, which allows the use of Microsoft Excel functions inside the code into the variable WF.

Set WF = Application.WorksheetFunction

Note: the variable WF is a variable that we created ourselves.

It is recommended to give variables a meaningful name. In this case, the variable name is composed of the initials of the object.

For example:

If we want to use Microsoft Excel functions in the code, we can write this:

Range("b1").Value = _

Application.WorksheetFunction.**Count**(Range("a1:a10"))

Range("b2").Value = _

Application.WorksheetFunction.**Average**(Range("a1:a10"))

Range("b3").Value = _

Application.WorksheetFunction.**Sum**(Range("a1:a10"))

However, if we make a one-time setting of the object Application.WorksheetFunction into the variable WF, we can write a shorter and more legible code:

Set WF = Application.WorksheetFunction

Range("b1").Value = WF.**Count**(Range("a1:a10"))

Range("b2").Value = WF.**Average**(Range("a1:a10"))

Range("b3").Value = WF.**Sum**(Range("a1:a10"))

Note: The functions Count, Average and Sum are written in bold in order to be easily identified by the readers of this book. In practice, they appear as regular text, not bold.

Cells and Ranges

Applying to Cells and Ranges

One of the basic actions in Microsoft Excel is applying to ranges on which we wish to conduct various processing.

A range can be a single cell, a sequence of cells, a column, a row, or even the entire worksheet.

The main commands related to ranges are:
- Range
- ActiveCell
- Selection

Examples:

Code	Action
Range("b5").Select	Selecting the cell B5 (Please note the quotation marks surrounding the cell name)
Range("b5:c10").Select	Selecting the range B5:C10
Range("b5", "c10").Select	Another way of applying to a range is by selecting its ends
Range("b5, c10").Select	Selecting non-sequential ranges
Range(ActiveCell, "d3").Select	Selecting a range from the Active Cell to cell D3

Range("first").Select	Selecting a range by using the name "first" that was given earlier to a cell or to a range of cells in the worksheet
Range("first", "Second").Select	Selecting a range by using two names that were given earlier to two cells in the worksheet
Selection.Interior.Color = vbGreen	Coloring in green a range of cells that were selected earlier in the worksheet/code

Note:

Although it seems that the command range("c2").select is selecting cell C2, in fact it is selecting the cell in the second row and the third column, as the default reference point is cell A1.

Therefore, the next command:

Range("b5").Range("a2").Select

Select the cell in the second row and the first column, according to the reference point B5, which means cell B6.

Useful commands for selecting ranges in Microsoft Excel

The following list of commands select ranges in the worksheet by using different keyboard shortcut keys.

The relevant VBA code is given alongside each command.

It is recommended to practice those commands in the worksheet itself, and also to record a macro and watch it.

- The shortcut key ctrl+down arrow ↓ will move the cursor from the active cell to the last cell in the column before the nearest empty cell:

```
ActiveCell.End(xlDown).Select
```

- The shortcut key shift+ctrl+down arrow ↓ will select the range from the active cell to the last cell in the column before the nearest empty cell:

```
Range(ActiveCell, ActiveCell.End(xlDown)).Select
```

- The shortcut key ctrl+up arrow ↑ will move the cursor to the first row in the data range that contains the active cell before the nearest empty cell (or to the top of the worksheet, if the first row of data is row number 1):

```
ActiveCell.End(xlUp).Select
```

- The shortcut key ctrl+shift+up arrow ↑ will select the entire range, from the cursor location up to the empty cell above it (or to the top of the worksheet, if the first row of data is row number 1):

```
Range(ActiveCell, ActiveCell.End(xlUp)).Select
```

- The shortcut key ctrl+right arrow → or left arrow ←will take the cursor to the first or the last data in a row (before the nearest empty cell), respectively:

```
ActiveCell.End(xlToRight).Select
ActiveCell.End(xlToLeft).Select
```

- The shortcut key ctrl+shift+ right arrow → or left arrow ← will select the data from the cursor location to the last cell in the column (before the nearest empty cell), from the right or from the left, respectively:

```
Range(ActiveCell, ActiveCell.End(xlToRight)).Select
```

- The shortcut key ctrl+asterisk (*) will select the data table. It is customary to use the asterisk (*) key from the numeric section of the keyboard, but if you choose to use the asterisk above the number 8 from the upper row of numbers in the alpha-numeric section of the keyboard, press on the Shift key as well (ctrl+shift+8):

```
ActiveCell.CurrentRegion.Select
```

- The shortcut key Ctrl+A will select the entire worksheet:

```
Cells.Select
```

- The shortcut key Ctrl+Home will move the cursor to cell A1:

```
Range("A1").Select
```

- The shortcut key Ctrl+End will move the cursor to the last data cell in the worksheet:

```
ActiveCell.SpecialCells(xlLastCell).Select
```

Tip:
To perform actions on the entire active data range in the worksheet, you can use the command UsedRange, for example:
ActiveSheet.UsedRange.Font.Size = 12

ActiveCell

This enables you to perform actions on the active cell, without mentioning its specific location.

For example

The command:

```
ActiveCell.Value = 5
```

74

enters the value 5 into the active cell (the cell which the cursor is in).

Rows

This enables you to refer to entire rows.

For example

The command:

```
Rows("2:3").Select
```

selects rows 2 to 3.

Columns

This enables you to refer to columns.

For example

The command:

```
Columns("C:D").Select
```

selects columns C to D.

EntireRow

This enables you to select the entire row that is related to a certain object.

For example

The command:

```
ActiveCell.EntireRow.Select
```

will select the entire row of the active cell

EntireColumn

This enables you to select the entire column that is related to a certain object.

For example

The command:

```
ActiveCell.EntireColumn.Interior.Color = vbRed
```

will color the entire column of the active cell in red.

Cells

This enables you to select a cell, using the row number and the column number. The importance of this command is that it enables you to refer to a cell in accordance with variables, and not with fixed data only:

```
Cells(row, column).Select
```

For example

The command:

```
Cells(5, 7).Select
```

selects cell G5.

Note:

In Microsoft Excel, the column number is specified first, followed by the row number. However, in the VB editor the row number should be specified first, followed by the column number.

Tip:

To select the last row in a contiguous data set (in column A, for example), use the following code:

```
Cells(Rows.Count, 1).End(xlUp).Select
```

Explanation:

The command Rows.Count returns the number of rows in the worksheet (in an xls file, the number of rows is 65,536; and in xlsx or xlsm files, it is 1,048,576).

Therefore, we have asked the program to go to the last cell of column A, and go up to the first row of data, from the bottom.

To use the row number, you must enter the code into a variable and ask for the row number instead of selecting it. For example:

LastRow = Cells(Rows.Count, 1).End(xlUp).Row

(LastRow is a variable. We will discuss variables later on in this book.)

Offset

This enables you refer to a cell, relative to the active cell.

The command structure:

Offset (rows, columns)

For example:

Range("c5").Offset(3, 2).Select

The above command selects the cell which is located three rows down and two columns to the right of cell C5; that is, cell E8.

ActiveCell.Offset(-3, 2).Interior.Color = vbRed

The above command colors the cell which is located three rows up and two columns to the right of the active cell.

Operations on ranges

Copy

The copy action is done by using the **copy** command:

```
Range("a3").Copy
```

Paste

The paste action is done by using the **ActiveSheet.Paste** command:

```
Range("a3").Copy
Range("a4").Select
ActiveSheet.Paste
Application.CutCopyMode = False
```

The above code copies the content of cell A3 and pastes it into cell A4.

The command: Application.CutCopyMode = False cancels the copying state (the surrounding lineal) of cell A3.

Tip:

You can use the following shortcut to paste the value into the desired range (in this case, into cell A4):

```
Range("a3").Copy Range("a4")
```

Alternatively, you can use the code:

```
Range("a4").Value = Range("a3").Value
```

Note:

Although both of the codes above yield the same result, the way they perform the action is completely different:

In the first code, we copied the value from cell A3 and pasted it into cell A4.

In the second code, we entered the value of cell A3 into cell A4 by using the "=" operation.

Naming a range

You can give names to cells or ranges from within the workbook itself, but you can also do it by using the command **Name**.

For example:

```
Range("a1:a5").Name = "FirstRange"

Range("FirstRange").Select
```

In this code, we gave the name "FirstRange" to the range A1:B5, and then we selected it according to its name.

Making calculations on ranges

You can perform mathematical calculations on cells, for example:

```
Range("a3").Value = Range("a3").Value - 3

Range("a4").Value = Range("a3").Value + 10
```

In the example above, cell A3 received a new value after a calculation that subtracted the number 3 from its current value.
Cell A4 received a value equal to the value in cell A3, plus 10.

Note:

In Microsoft Excel you cannot enter a value into a cell that is based on a calculation that includes the cell itself ("circular reference"). However, it is possible when writing a VBA code, because the result of the calculation will appear in the cell as a value and not as a formula.

Exercise:

1. Open the workbook "**Select Ranges.xls**".
2. Write a macro for selecting the following ranges:
   a. the entire table
   b. the data in column A
   c. the data in the third row
   d. Range A2:C3

Sheets

This chapter deals with the main command related to working with sheets.

Selecting Sheets

You can address a sheet by its name:

```
Sheets("data").Select
```

Or by its serial number in the worksheet:

```
Sheets(2).Select
```

Tip:

Use the following code to select the last sheet in the workbook:

```
Sheets(Sheets.Count).Select
```

Explanation:

The command **Sheets.Count** returns the number of sheets in the workbook.

Therefore, in this code we have asked to select the sheets that its serial number equals to the number of sheets in the workbook.

Referring to the current sheet

This is done with the **ActiveSheet** command.

For example:

```
ActiveSheet.Delete
```

Please note: to avoid the message that appears while deleting a sheet, use the '**Preventing alerts**' tip, on page 148.

Adding sheets

This is done with the following command:

83

```
Sheets.add
```

To determine the location of the sheet to be added:

```
Sheets.Add before:=Sheets(3)
```

Adding a sheet after the last sheet:

```
Sheets.Add after:=Sheets(Sheets.Count)
```

Moving a sheet to another location in the file

```
Sheets(3).Move Before:=Sheets(1)
```

Moving a sheet to a new workbook

```
Sheets(1). Move
```

Moving a sheet to an existing workbook

Note: the destination file should be open:

```
Sheets(2).Move Before:=Workbooks("My WB.xlsx").Sheets(1)
```

Copying a sheet

```
Sheets(3).Copy Before:=Sheets(1)
```

Copying a sheet to another workbook

Note: the destination file should be open:

```
Sheets(1).Copy Before:=Workbooks("My WB.xlsx").Sheets(1)
```

Changing a sheet's name

```
Sheets(1).Name = "NewName"
```

Tip:

You can add a new worksheet and set its name with one command:

```
Sheets.Add.Name = "Data"
```

Changing the tab's color

```
ActiveSheet.Tab.Color = vbRed
```

Variables

A variable is a kind of "memory stack" whose purpose is to store data temporarily.

The "stack" contents can change while the code is running.

It is customary to declare the names and also the types of variables at the beginning of the code.

Rules for naming variables:

- A variable name must start with a letter.
- The name of a variable cannot contain spaces.
- You cannot use the same name as the name of the macro.
- You cannot use reserved names such as 'save' and 'print'.
  To avoid problems arising from the use of reserved names, you can add the suffix 'My' to the variable name, for example – MySum.
- It is recommended to use a name which accurately describes the meaning of the variable. For example, name the variable that stores the number of the last row in a specific column 'LastRow'.
- You can use the underscore to combine two words, for example, Last_Row. It is customary to use lowercase and uppercase letters to make reading easier.

- An incorrectly typed variable will create a new variable. For example: let's say you gave a variable the name MyRng and later on you mistakenly wrote MyRange; a new variable with this name would be created automatically.

- Before the code starts running, the variables get a primary value. Variables that were declared as numeric will get the

---

value 0, and variables that were declared as a string (text) will get the value "empty".

- When you stop running the code, the value of the variable is automatically reset and is not saved in the memory (in other words, when the code stops running, all the "memory stacks" are emptied of their contents).

Note:

Naming a variable with an illegal name will color the line in red.

Types of Variables

There are many types of variables. We will discuss only the most important ones:

Numeric variable

Variable Type	Size (Bytes)	Values Range
Byte	1	0 to 255
Boolean	2	True or False
Integer	2	(-32,768) to (32,767)
Long	4	(-2,147,483,648) to (2,147,483,647)

Other variables

Double – Allows storing of the decimal numbers.

String – Allows storing of the text strings.

Range – Allows storing of the ranges.

Date – Allows storing of the dates.

Variant – "super variable" – stores all of above variables in it.

However, to save memory space, use the smallest variable type that can do the job for you, so that it doesn't eat up the memory available.

Note: you do not have to declare variables, but if they are not declared, the variable type might be determined as VARIANT by default, which uses a lot of memory space.

To obligate the users to declare variables in a certain module, you can add the command **'Option Explicit'** at the top of the module, which will prevent the code from running if there are undeclared variables.

Declaration of variables is done by the command **Dim**.

For example:

```
Dim LastRow As Integer
Dim Rng As Range
```

In this code we defined the variable LastRow as an Integer, while the variable Rng was defined as a Range.

Why should you obligate the user to declare variables?

Although it is not mandatory to declare variables, avoiding the declaration can cause problems due to the fact that each time the compiler encounters a variable it does not recognize, it creates a new one.

The next example will help to clarify this:

We have a product at a certain price, and we wish to raise the price by 10%. We have to multiply the old price by 1.1, therefore we wrote the following code:

```
OldPrice = 30
NewPrice = price * 1.1
```

We gave the variable OldPrice a primary value of 30.

Then, we wanted to get the new value of the product in the variable NewPrice, but didn't realize we had used the variable Price instead of OldPrice.

Due to the fact that the variable Price is unrecognized, it is automatically created and receives the default value 0; therefore the multiplication result is 0 and not 33 as expected.

If the user were obligated to declare variables, we would get an error message when the compiler encountered the variable Price.

You can declare a variable without declaring its type:

Dim LastRow

In this case the editor will prevent us from using the variables incorrectly, but the variable type will be determined as a Variant, which uses a lot of memory space.

Viewing the variables whilst running the code

Whilst running the code in a 'step-by-step' mode, you can view the values that each variable receives.

Locals window

This displays a list of all the variables in the procedure.

To show the window, select **View → Locals Window**:

Expression	Value	Type
⊞ Module1		Module1/Module1
i	1	Variant/Integer
j	51	Variant/Integer

You can see the variables change during the running of the code in a '**step-by-step**' mode.

Watch window

This enables you to view the selected variables while the code is running.

Add variables to the window:

1. Right-click on the desired variable (from within the code).

2. Select Add Watch:

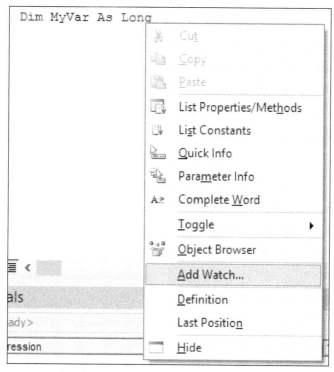

3. The following window will open:

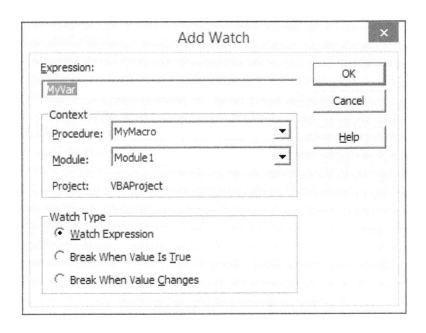

4. Make sure you selected the right variable.

5. Click [OK]

6. The variable will appear in the window, as shown in the illustration below:

Watches			
Expression	Value	Type	Context
66 MyVar	5	Long	Module1.MyMacro

'With' Command

Sometimes we are required to perform several actions on the same range.

In this case, we can write a macro like the one in the following example, which performs four different actions on the cell A1:

```
Range("a1").Interior.Color = vbYellow

Range("a1").Font.Bold = True

Range("a1").Font.Color = vbRed

Range("a1").Value = Range("a1").Value * 2
```

However, the VB editor enables you to write more clearly and briefly by using the "**With**" Command. This assigns all the commands to the selected object, specifying its name only once.

Syntax:

```
With Object
        .command1
        .command2
End With
```

```
Note the dot (.) at the beginning of each command line.
```

```
With Range("a1")
        vbYellow = roloC.roiretnI.
        .Font.Bold = True
        .Font.Color = vbRed
        .Value = Range("a1").Value * 2
End With
```

In the sample above, we referred to cell A1 only once, and then performed different actions on it.

In terms of results, there is no difference between the first code and the second one, but the second code saves typing and looks clearer.

Strings

Strings are textual sequences on which you can make different manipulations.

Syntax rules:

- Each string will be surrounded by quotation marks. For example: "Hello".
- Strings concatenation, or concatenating a string to a variable, will be done by the symbol "&", For example: "hello " & "goodbye".

Important commands for strings:

Len - returns the string length.

Syntax:

Len (text)

Example:

To return the length of the string Hello World:

```
MyLen = Len("Hello World")
```

To return the length of the string in cell C3:

```
MyLen = Len(Range("c3"))
```

Ucase – Converts the letters of the string into uppercase.

Syntax:

Ucase (text)

Example:

The code:

```
ActiveCell.Value = UCase(ActiveCell.Value)
```

Converts the letters of the string into uppercase, in the active cell.

LCase - converts the letters of the string into lowercase.

Syntax:

Lcase (text)

Left – returns a fixed number of characters from the left side of the string.

Syntax:

Left (text, length)
Example:

Return to cell A2 five characters from the left side of the string in cell A1:

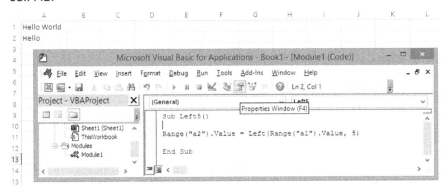

Right – returns a fixed number of characters from the right side of the string.

Syntax:

Right (text, length)

Mid – returns a fixed number of characters from the middle of the string.

Syntax:

Mid (text, start , length)

Note that the 'length' argument specifies the desired length of the returned string, and it is optional. If it is omitted, the string that will be returned is the one that starts from the place specified in the second argument, and ends at the last character of the string.

Instr – returns the position of one string inside another string.
Syntax:
Instr (start, where, what)

For example:

Find the 'space' character location inside the string "Hello World":

```
MySpace = InStr(1, "Hello World", " ")
```

The variable MySpace will get the value 6, because the 'space' character is the sixth character of the string "Hello World".

Instead of writing the string in a code line, you can refer the search to a cell in the worksheet:

```
MySpace = InStr(1, Range("a1"), " ")
```

InStrRev – returns the location of one string inside another, when the search begins from the end of the string.
Syntax:
InStrRev (where, what, start)

For example:
Search for the letter "o" in the string "Hello World", beginning from the end:

```
MyO = InStrRev("Hello World", "o")
```

Note: the search is done from the end of the string, but the result is the location from the beginning of the string, and in this case, the variable MyO will receive the value 8.

You can also refer the search to a cell in the worksheet, instead of writing the string inside the code.

Replace – replaces one string with another.

Syntax:

Replace (string, sub-string to replace, replace with)
For example:

Replace the word 'big' with the word 'small':

```
MyRplc = Replace("I'm Big", "Big", "Small")
```

You can also refer the search to a cell in the worksheet, instead of writing the string inside the code.

Date and Time

Dates are stored in the VB editor as decimal numbers, starting from the January 1st 100 till December 31st 9999.

Note: although the VB editor recognizes dates from the year 100, Microsoft Excel itself does not recognize dates prior to the year 1900.

When you enter a date composed of numerals, surround it with the symbol #:

```
MyDt = #12/31/2016#
```

When you enter a date as a string, surround it with double quotes:

```
MyDt = "December 31, 2016"
```

The command that returns today's date is **Date** (this is equal to the function '**Today()**' in Microsoft Excel).
The following code will enter today's date into cell A1:

```
Range("a1").Value = Date
```

The following code will calculate the date that occurs in 7 days from today, and enter it into cell A1:

```
Range("a1").Value = Date + 7
```

Time

This command returns the time.
The following code will enter the time into the variable MyTm:

```
MyTm = Time
```

TimeSerial

This command returns the time in an hours:minutes:seconds structure.

Syntax:

TimeSerial(hh, mm, ss)

The following code returns the time 1:25:00 into the variable MyTm:

```
MyTm = TimeSerial(1, 25, 0)
```

The following code returns the time that will apply, three hours, twenty minutes and fifteen seconds from now, into the variable MyTm:

```
MyTm = Now + TimeSerial(3, 20, 15)
```

Interaction With the User

One of the most powerful options of VB editor is the ability to interact with the user while running the code, by displaying messages to the user and receiving inputs from the user.

MsgBox

A message box is used to display messages to the user.

Syntax:

```
MsgBox ("Enter your text here")
```

Example:

```
MsgBox ("Hello")
```

Useful symbols for the MsgBox

The symbol "&" is concatenating text strings.

As in the following code, for example:

```
MsgBox ("Hello " & Application.UserName)
```

The following message will appear:

Note the space after the word "Hello ".

The space was added inside the quotation marks after the word "Hello", in order to add a space between the two parts of the message.

The command **Appliction.UserName** returns the username that was set during the installation of the Microsoft Excel package.

The command VbNewLine allows the creation of a new row inside the message box.

For example:

MsgBox ("Hello" & vbNewLine & Application.UserName)

The following message will appear:

100

You can also use chr(10) in order to create a new line:

```
MsgBox ("Hello " & Chr(10) & Application.UserName)
```

A message box that allows decision-making

As we saw, the message box allows the user to receive messages. However, you can use the message box to enable the user to choose between several existing options, such as "OK" or "Cancel". Because in this type of message box, we receive information from the user, we have to store it in a variable for a future use.

Syntax:

MyMsg = MsgBox ("Your Text", vbButtons)

For example:

```
msginfo = MsgBox("Do you want to proceed?", vbYesNo)
If msginfo = vbNo Then
        Exit Sub
End If
```

In the example above we used a message box of vbYesNo type, which displays two option buttons:

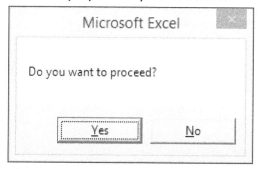

The returned value will be entered into the variable MsgInfo.

Now we can act according to the result received in the variable, usually by using the command If (which will be taught in the next chapter).

Button options:

- vbOKOnly
- vbOKCancel
- vbAbortRetryIgnore
- vbYesNoCancel
- vbYesNo
- vbRetryCancel

Warning options:

- vbCritical

- vbExclamation

- vbInformation

Note:

Warning options are used for display purposes only!

You can combine buttons and warnings inside a message box:

MyMsg = MsgBox("Quit Without Saving?", vbOKCancel + vbExclamation)

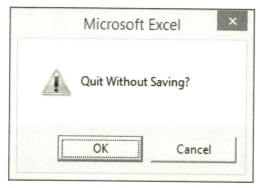

Pay attention to the "+" symbol that is used to connect the two options!

InputBox

InputBox is used to receive information from the user.

The information will be stored in a variable for future use.

The command structure:

MyVar = InputBox ("Your Text")

For example:

```
UsrNm = InputBox("What is your name?")
```

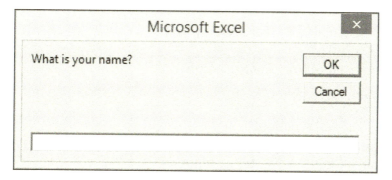

The following code requests the user to enter his/her name, and then returns a message box with the value that the user entered into the variable UsrNm:

```
UsrNm = InputBox ("What Is Your Name?")
MsgBox ("Hello " & UsrNm)
```

Explanation:

The value that was entered by the user using the InputBox will be entered into the variable UsrNm.

In the second stage, a message will be displayed to the user by the MsgBox command, showing the concatenation of the string "Hello" with the value that was stored in the variable UsrNm.

Please note, when entering numbers to the InputBox, they will be defined as strings and not as a number, i.e – when entering the number 5, for example, the variable will get the value "5" (text string).

There are several ways to deal with it:

⬚   Define the variable as a numeric variable:

```
Dim MyNum As Integer
MyNum = InputBox ("Enter a number")
```

- Make a calculation that does not change the value (for example, add 0 or multiply by 1):

```
MyNum = InputBox ("Enter a number")
MyNum = MyNum * 1
```

- Use Val function:

```
MyNum = InputBox ("Enter a number")
MyNum = Val (MyNum)
```

Adding a title to the InputBox:

To change the title from the 'Microsoft Excel' default title, use the following code:

```
UsrNm = InputBox("What Is Your Name?", "Names")
```

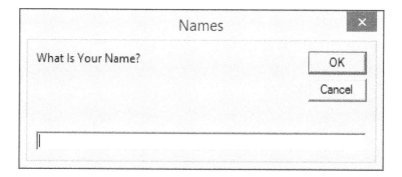

Conditions

Conditions allow you to make decisions based on data obtained while running the code.

The basic condition command structure

If condition then

        Commands for execution

End if

Meaning: the condition is examined to see whether it received a "True" or "False" value. The operating instructions will apply only if the value "True" was received.

Comparison operators

Operators	Meaning
=	Equal to
<>	Not equal to
>	Bigger than...
<	Smaller than...
>=	Bigger than or equal to...
<=	Smaller than or equal to...
And	Gets "True" value only when all parts of the equation are satisfied
Or	Gets "True" value when one part or both parts of the equation are satisfied

Operators	Meaning
=	Equal to
<>	Not equal to
>	Bigger than...
<	Smaller than...
Not	Gets "True" value only when the relevant part of the equation is not satisfied

Examples:

The following code checks whether the value in cell A1 is bigger than the value in cell A2.

If it is bigger, a message box will appear, indicating "a1 is bigger than a2".

```
If Range("a1").Value > Range("a2").Value Then

        MsgBox ("a1 is bigger than a2")

End If
```

The above code checks the truth of the statement A1>A2. If it is - meaning that the value in cell A1 is actually bigger than the value in cell A2 - the operating instructions will be carried out and, in this case, a text box with the sentence "a1 is bigger than a2" will appear.

If it is a false sentence, meaning that the value in cell A1 is not bigger than the value in cell A2, the message box will not appear.

Note: testing conditions is not limited to numeric values only.

The following code checks whether the username that was entered is Jenny. In the event that it is, a message will appear.

```
UsrName = InputBox("What is your name?")

If UsrName = "Jenny" Then

        MsgBox ("Hello Jenny ")

End If
```

Note: text comparison is case sensitive. Therefore, if the name "JENNY" was entered, the condition would get the value "false"; after all, we compared it to the string "Jenny". Therefore, contrary to our expectations, the desired text box will not appear.

We can solve it in two ways:

- Comprehensively - by adding the command **Option Compare Text** at the top of the module, which will cancel the case sensitivity of all module codes.

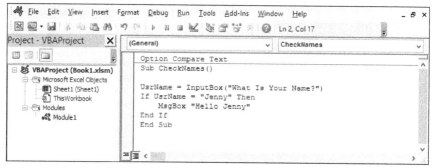

- For a specific command – by using **LCase** or **UCase** to convert both strings to the same case.

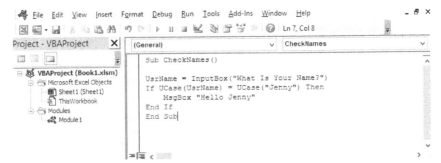

Choosing which approach to take depends on the purpose of the strings comparison. If, in most parts of the code, the letter type is important, then it is better to avoid using the command Option Compare Text, which would cancel the case sensitivity of all module commands.

Complex condition

Sometimes we will have to execute one kind of instruction when the condition is "True" and a different instruction when it is "False". For that, we must use the structure:

If... Then... Else

Syntax:

If condition Then

      Commands for execution

Else

      Commands for execution

End if

Example:

In the following code, we ask the user to enter his/her name. If the name entered is Jenny, the user will get the message "Hi Jenny". If a different name is entered, the message will be "I wish you were Jenny":

110

```
UsrName = InputBox("What is your name?")

If UsrName = "Jenny" Then

   MsgBox ("Hi Jenny")

Else

   MsgBox ("I wish you were Jenny")

End If
```

When more than two conditions exist, you can use ElseIf.

Example:

```
UsrName = InputBox("What is your name?")
If UsrName = " Jenny" Then
        MsgBox "Hi Jenny"
ElseIf UsrName = "Dan" Then
        MsgBox "Hi Dan"
Else
        MsgBox "I wish you were Jenny"
End If
```

Example for using VbButtons:

```
Prcd = MsgBox("Do you want to proceed?", vbYesNo)

If Prcd = vbYes Then

   ActiveCell.Value = 5

End If
```

Explanation:

The value that was chosen by the VbYesNo button was entered into the variable Prcd.

If the user clicked 'Yes', the value 5 would be entered into the active cell (and if 'No' was clicked, nothing would happen). Loops

111

One of the most useful tools of code-writing is the loop structure, which enables the code to be run a number of times in succession, according to the data entered.

For example, if we have a large database, and we want to run a test on a large number of data records, we can write a code line for each data record. However, it is easier and more efficient to write the code line only once and run it in a loop over all of the data records.

There are two main loop types:

- The Do loop type, which allows the code to be repeated under certain conditions.
- The For loop type, which allows the code to be repeated a pre-determined number of times.

Do-Loop

This loop enables the same code lines to be repeated under certain conditions, when the number of repetitions is unknown.

There are two types of Do-Loop loops.

Do-While loop

This loop enables the same code lines to be repeated as long as a certain condition exists.

```
Range("a1").Select
Do While ActiveCell.Value <> ""
    ActiveCell.Value = ActiveCell.Value * 2
    ActiveCell.Offset(1, 0).Select
Loop
```

Explanation:

In the above example, the code multiplies the value of the active cell by 2, then selects the cell below it and multiplies it, and so on, as long as the active cell is not empty.

If an empty cell is selected while the code is running, the code will stop running (even if other cells with values are located below the empty cell).

Do-Until loop

This loop enables the same code lines to be repeated until a certain condition occurs.

```
Range("a1").Select
Do Until ActiveCell.Value = ""
        ActiveCell.Value = ActiveCell.Value * 2
        ActiveCell.Offset(1, 0).Select
Loop
```

Explanation:

In the above example, the code multiplies the active cell value by 2, then selects the cell below it and multiplies it, and so on, until it meets at an empty cell.

When an empty cell is reached, the code will stop running (even if other cells with values are located below the empty cell).

In effect, both codes are performing the same action, but with a different approach. In the first code, the condition is: as long as the cell is not empty, and in the second code the condition is: until it meets an empty cell.

For-loop

This loop allows a code to be repeated a pre-determined number of times.

The loop structure:
For counter = X To Y
      Commands for execution
Next counter

Example:

```
For i = 1 To 10
      MsgBox (i)
Next i
```

The above loop uses the variable "i" to receive values from 1-10. Each time the variable gets value, a message box with the value of the variable appears.

By default, the loop counter increases by 1 each time, but you can set the number of "steps" by using the command Step:

```
For i = 2 To 10 Step 2
      MsgBox (i)
Next i
```

Another example:

```
For i = 10 To 2 Step -2
      MsgBox (i)
Next i
```

Please note the minus (-) sign when stepping backwards.

Example for creating the multiplication table by using a 'For' loop:

```
For i = 1 To 10

   For j = 1 To 10

      Cells(i, j) = i * j

   Next j

Next i
```

Explanation:

In this code there are two variables: "i" and "j", which receive values from 1 to 10.

Moreover, there are two For loops: internal and external.

Every time the external loop (i) counter increases by 1, the internal loop (j) runs 10 times and enters the multiplication of the variables "i" and "j" into the cell, the position of which is determined by the variables "i" and "j" values.

The following table will help you understand:

i	j	i*j
1	1	1
1	2	2
1	3	3
1	4	4
1	5	5
1	6	6
1	7	7
1	8	8
1	9	9
1	10	10
2	1	2
2	2	4
2	3	6
2	4	8
2	5	10
2	6	12
2	7	14
2	8	16
2	9	18
2	10	20

Recommendation:

Run the following code step-by-step and use the Watch window to see the changes of the values.

Note that there is no need to select the cell by using the command select in order to insert a value into it!

(In fact, one of the differences between an experienced programmer and a novice is the number of times the command select...is used.)

Tip:
You can use variables to determine beginning and end values:

```
ShtCnt = Sheets.Count
For i = 1 To ShtCnt
        Sheets(i).Range("a1").Value = Sheets(i).Name
Next i
```

Explanation

In the above example we used the variable ShtCnt to determine the number of worksheets in the workbook. Then we used the For-Next loop, which ran as many times as the number of worksheets and fed its name into cell A1, at each of the worksheets.

For-Each loop

The For-Each loop allows the performance of actions on collections, which gather objects of the same type.

A collection of worksheets, for example, gathers all of the worksheets in it; a collection of charts, gathers all of the charts in it; a range gathers cells in it and so on.

Syntax:

For each object in collection
        Commands for execution
Next

Creating a multiplication table by using a For-Each loop:

```
For Each CL In Range("a1:j10")
        CL.Value = CL.Row * CL.Column
Next
```

Explanation:

In this command, the macro goes through each of the cells in the specified range and multiplies the row number of the cell by its column number.

The VB editor "knows" that the object that builds the collection "range" is a cell, therefore it "understands" that the variable CL represents a "cell". Therefore, for the collection's objects, you can use any name (as long as it is not a reserved name, and preferably a meaningful one), in order to represent them.

In the same way, we gave the object that builds the collection of worksheets the name SH (which stands for a single worksheet).

```
For Each SH In Sheets
        SH.Tab.ColorIndex = 40
Next
```

The macro above colors the tab of the workbook pink.

Feeding the worksheet name into cell A1:

```
For Each SH In Sheets
        SH.Range("a1").Value = SH.Name
Next
```

As you see, in some cases you can choose between a For-Next loop or a For-Each loop to execute the same actions.

Using the For-Each loop is usually shorter and more elegant.

Files and Folders

So far, most of the book chapters have been directly related to the functions of Excel.

This chapter differs from the preceding chapters in that the functions which will be taught are mostly the connection between Excel and the operating system which provides the infrastructure to manage files: from saving files, to the creation of folders, deleting files and more.

Files

Opening a File

One common requirement is file opening.

Opening files using VBA can be done with a code that uses the name of the file and its path (assuming that they are already known), or by requesting the user to select the desired file using a dialog window.

Opening a File with Code

Workbooks.open command allows you to open a file using its name and the location where it's saved.

Syntax

```
Workbooks.Open ("FileToOpen")
```

Example

```
Workbooks.Open ("C:\Users\user\Documents \MyFile.xlsx")
```

The command above will open the file MyFile.xlsx that's saved at the path C:\Users\user\Documents.

The file name string can be entered directly in the code, or obtained from other sources as shown in the following example:

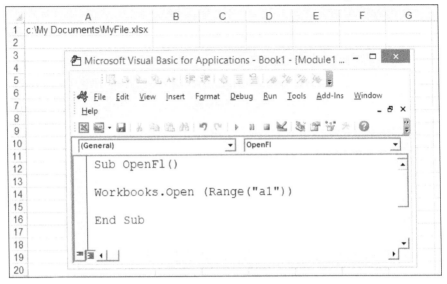

Show 'Open File' dialogue

Allows the user to select the desired file, from the "opening a file" window.

This function is more dynamic than the previous one, because it allows you to open another file each time, as needed, without changing the code. This means it requires user involvement whilst running the code.

Syntax:

```
Application.Dialogs(xlDialogOpen).Show
```

The following window will pop up:

120

The user must navigate to the appropriate folder, select the desired file, and finally click on

Saving the file name to a variable

This command is similar to the previous command, and displays the 'Open a dialog' to select the desired file. However, unlike the previous code, it does not open the file, but keeps its name in memory for future use.

Syntax

```
MyFile = Application.GetOpenFilename
```

Example

```
MyFile = Application.GetOpenFilename
Workbooks.Open MyFile
```

On the first row we asked to insert the file name that the user chooses into the variable MyFile, and at the second line we opened it with the command **Workbooks.Open**

The code also allows us to reduce the file list that appears in the window by selecting a filter. For example, to select only Excel files:

Syntax

```
Application.GetOpenFilename ("Excel Files (*.xlsx), *.xlsx")
```

> **Note:**
>
> The procedure of opening and saving files is part of the operating system which provides services to Excel. Therefore, certain commands may work in some operating systems and not others.

Saving a file

Our Excel files can be saved by code under the same file name and path, or with a new name and path.

Save

The basic saving command lets you save a previously stored file with the same name and location.

Syntax

```
ActiveWorkbook.Save
```

Save as

This command lets you save a file with a different name and/or a different path.

Syntax

```
ActiveWorkbook.SaveAs Filename:="MyFile", FileFormat:=x
```

This command has two criteria: Filename property sets the path and file name, and FileFormat property, which allows you to determine the file type, and has several fixed options:

Type	Number
xlsx	51

xlsm	52
xls	56
csv	5
pdf	57
txt	20

Example

```
ActiveWorkbook.SaveAs Filename:="D:\MyFile.xlsm",
FileFormat:=52
```

At the example above, we wanted to save the file named MyFile to drive D, and we set the file type to xlsm using the attribute Fileformat.

We kept the same as a pdf file with the following code:

```
ActiveWorkbook.SaveAs Filename:="D:\MyFile.pdf", FileFormat:=57
```

Please note, in order to save a file as PDF, you must make sure that there is at least one cell containing information.

Deleting a file

This is done by using the Kill command.

Deleting a file:

```
Kill "D:\MyFile.xlsm"
```

Deleting all the files in the folder:

```
Kill "D:\My Folder\*.*"
```

Checking if a file exists:

```
If Dir("D:\MyFile.xlsx") = "" Then

   MsgBox ("File doesn't exist ")

End If
```

Folders

Creating a folder

Is done with the command MkDir

```
MkDir "D:\My New Folder"
```

Getting the current folder path

Is done with the command:

```
CurDir
```

Deleting an empty folder

```
RmDir "D:\My New Folder"
```

Checking if a folder exists

```
If Dir("D:\My New Folder", vbDirectory) = "" Then

   MsgBox ("The folder does not exist ")

End If
```

User Defined Functions

Using VBA programming enables us to develop our own functions to use with Microsoft Excel.

The function purpose is to return a value, and it must be written at the module level (and not at the worksheet level).

If you wish your functions to be available to all workbooks and not just the current one, you should save them in the Personal.xlsb .

> Note that the 'Personal.xlsb' workbook does not exist until you record a macro and save it in that workbook. After this one-time action, the recorded macro can be deleted, and you can save all the functions that you want to be available for all workbooks.

Syntax:

Function function name (x, y)

      Commands for execution

End Function

Explanation:

Unlike codes, which begin with the word Sub, functions begin with the keyword **Function** and end with the phrase End Function.

Enter the number of possible arguments in the brackets.

The following example shows a developed function that divides two variables:

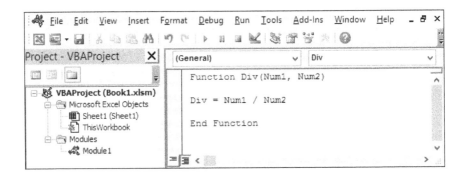

Explanation:

We tell the VB editor that we are about to write a function named Div, which has two arguments (Num1, Num2).

Then, we define the action (operation) that we want to perform on those variables.

> **Note**:
>
> The name of the function must be identical to that of the variable where the result will be inserted (contrary to routines, where variable names must be different from that of the routine itself).

Saving place to optional arguments

Sometimes we have to make calculations with an unknown number of arguments.

Suppose we have to add 2 or 3 numbers.

The following code:

```
Function plus(Num1, Num2)

  plus = Num1 + Num2

End Function
```

will allow us to use only 2 arguments.

Whereas the next code:

```
Function plus(Num1, Num2, Num3)

  plus = Num1 + Num2 + Num3

End Function
```

will force us to use 3 arguments.

The solution is to define the 3rd argument as optional, and deal with it inside the code, as you can see in the following example:

```
Function plus(Num1, Num2, Optional Num3)

If IsMissing(Num3) Then

  Num3= 0

End If

plus = Num1 + Num2 + Num3

End Function
```

How to run the function from a Microsoft Excel workbook

There are two ways to run the function:

By the Insert function button:

1. Select tab **Formulas → Insert** function:

2. Select the category **User Defined**:

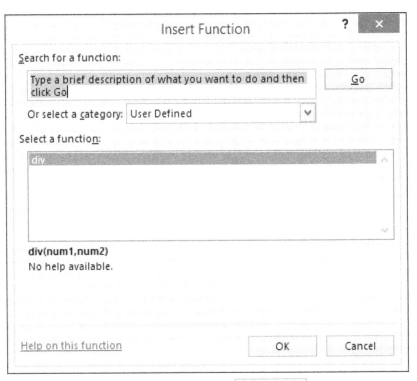

3. Select the function and click [OK]

4. The following window will open:

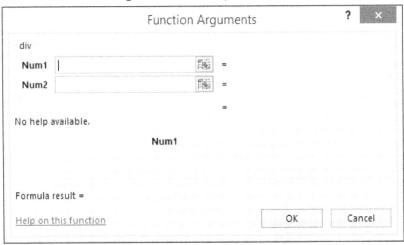

5. In this window, enter the relevant values or references.

128

6. To finish, click [OK]

By directly typing the function name in the worksheet:

	A
1	10
2	2
3	=Div(A1,A2)

Tip:

You cannot check a function by running it directly from the VB editor, but you can add a breakpoint at the beginning of the function and then run it from the workbook.

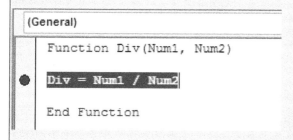

```
(General)

    Function Div(Num1, Num2)

●   Div = Num1 / Num2

    End Function
```

In this way, the function execution will stop, the VB editor will open and then you can continue running it using either F5 or F8.

When the test finishes, don't forget to remove the breakpoint.

Error handling

There are three main types of errors handled by the software.

- **Syntax Error** – this appears when the code doesn't follow the VBA syntax rules. In this case, the line will be colored in red.

  In the following example, the second code line was colored in red, since the user forgot the quotation mark after the cell name.

```
Sub MyErrors()
range("a1).select
End Sub
```

  We must detect the problem that caused the error by ourselves.

- **Compilation Error** – this appears when the command structure is wrong. For example, a For loop without the suffix Next, or If command without the ending line End IF.

  In the following example, we wrote a For loop, but we haven't closed it with the Next command. While trying to run the code, this error message will appear:

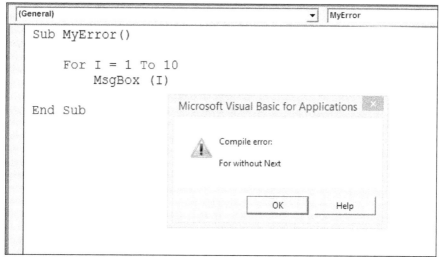

Note, the compiler checks the code before it starts running.

- **Run-Time Error** – this appears while the code is running, as a reaction to a command that cannot be performed, such as referring to a worksheet that does not exist. When this kind of error is detected, the code stops running and an error message appears.

In the following example, we tried to select the cell above the active cell. When we selected cell A1, we received an error message, because there are no cells above it.

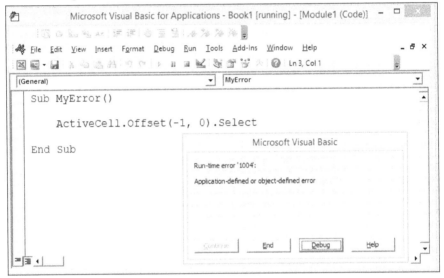

As we have seen, in that command there was neither a syntax error nor an error in structure; therefore we were unable to detect the problem before running the code.

Handling Run-time errors is done by the command On Error.

On Error GoTo Label

This command refers to another part in the code which is supposed to handle that kind of error.

```
On Error GoTo line1

ActiveCell.Offset(-1, 0).Select

Exit Sub

line1:

If ActiveCell.Row = 1 Then

MsgBox "First Line"

End If
```

In the above code, we refer the editor to the label 'line1' where we will display a message box to the user which clarifies that he is in the first row.

Note: because the code is running linearly, it will continue running to "line1" according to the order of the code lines, even if no error was detected. In the above example, a message box will appear. Therefore, we added the command Exit Sub after the appropriate cell selection, which causes the code to stop running.

Although you can "jump" from one part to another while running the code, it is recommended to use this option only for handling errors, since it makes the code complicated to understand.

To be able to "jump", you must add the code label with a colon at the end, and call it by name with the command GoTo, as shown in the example above.

On error resume next

In some cases we would like to comprehensively ignore Run-time errors.

To do so, we will write the command **On error resume next** before a line that might contain an error. This will instruct the compiler to ignore errors, even if they exist.

Be sure to use this option only when you are prepared to accept the errors that will arise while the code is running.

Sometimes we might want to use this command in one part of the code, but not in other parts.

To cancel the command, use the command On Error GoTo 0.

An Event Macro

The VBA is an event-oriented language.

An event macro enables a macro to run automatically following certain events made in the workbook, such as opening, closing, saving, double-clicking, changing and more.

A macro of this kind is written at the worksheet level or at the workbook level (ThisWorkbook in the explorer), and not at the module level.

An event macro written at the worksheet level will apply only to the worksheet it was written in, while an event macro at the workbook level will apply to all the worksheets in the file.

Note:
The macro names are pre-determined and cannot be changed.

An event macro at the worksheet level

1. Double-click the name of the desired worksheet in the object explorer:

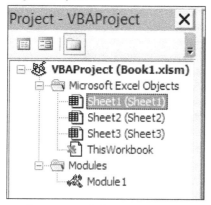

2. In the upper-left window select WorkSheet:

3. Choose the event that will run the code automatically from a list in the right window.

The following table lists the important events in the worksheet:

Macro	Action
Change	This macro will run automatically when a value in one of the worksheet cells changes
SelectionChange	This macro will run automatically when cells in the worksheet are selected

Note: when selecting an event macro of Change type, the reserved word Target will appear inside the brackets.

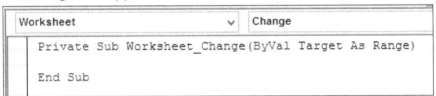

Target represents the range that triggered the event (contrary to ActiveCell that represents the active cell).

Run the following code to see the difference between Target and ActiveCell:

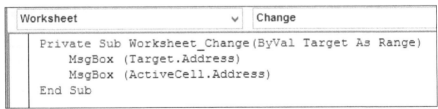

An event macro at the workbook level

1. Double-click ThisWorkBook:

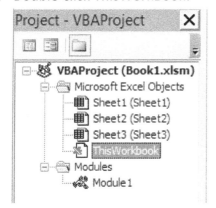

2. In the left upper window, select Workbook:

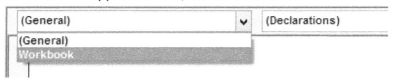

3. Choose the event which will run the code automatically from the list in the right window.

The following table lists the important events in the workbook:

Macro	Action
Open	This macro will run automatically when you open the workbook
BeforeClose	This macro will run before the file is closed (it enables the running of tests which prevent the file from being closed if pre-determined conditions were not fulfilled)
NewSheet	This macro will run when a new worksheet is added
BeforeSave	This macro will run before the file is saved

Deactivate	This macro will run when the workbook will become non-active (for example, when selecting a different file)
SheetChange	This macro will run when a change occurs in one of the worksheets

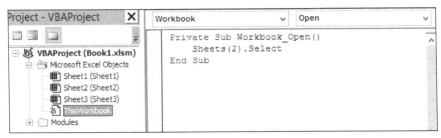

The above event macro is the Workbook_open type; in other words, this macro runs when the workbook is opened.

In this case, when the file opens, the second worksheet will open automatically.

Tip:

The following code cancels the workbook closure:

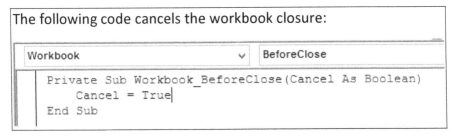

Supplements

How to protect the code from being viewed or copied

This protection blocks the unauthorized user from entering the code, looking at it or editing it.

1. Right-click on the project window (you can click anywhere in the project area).

2. Select VBAProject Properties.

3. In the open window, select the Protection tab:

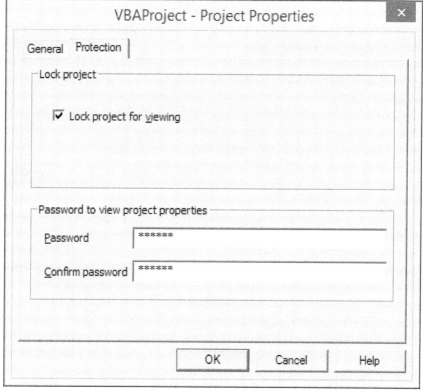

4. Check 'Lock project for viewing'.

5. Enter password.

6. Any attempt to enter the VBA editor will open a window requesting a password:

> **Note**:
> The protection will only take effect after closing and reopening the file.

Recommendation:

> It is recommended to use a password that you can easily remember when you will try to view the code in the future...

Increase the macro running speed

Long codes that work on a large range of data slow the computer processing power.

One of the main reasons for that is that every action executed while the code is running actually takes place on the screen.

It is possible to make the code run without the screen refreshing:

At the beginning of the code write the command:

```
Application.ScreenUpdating = False
```

Don't forget to return the screen to refresh at the end of the code by the command:

```
Application.ScreenUpdating = True
```

Calling a macro from another macro

You can run a macro from another macro. The call is made by writing the second code name inside the current one.

For example:

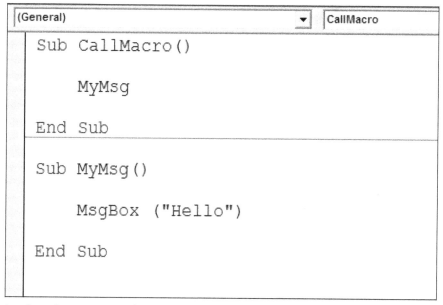

```
(General)                                    ▼    CallMacro

   Sub CallMacro()

       MyMsg

   End Sub

   Sub MyMsg()

       MsgBox ("Hello")

   End Sub
```

In the above example, running the code CallMacro, which calls the code MyMsg, will display a text box with the word "Hello".

Using the Microsoft Excel functions in a macro

Sometimes we want to use Excel functions in the macro we write. It is done by the **Application.WorksheetFunction** code, followed by the desired function name.

For example:

```
Range("a11").Value = _

Application.WorksheetFunction.Average(Range("a1:a10"))
```

Using colors

There are a few methods for choosing a color:

- By using the color name, for example vbRed.
- By using the index number of the color, for example ColorIndex=3:

```
Range("a1").Interior.Color = vbRed

Range("a2").Interior.ColorIndex = 26

Range("a3").Font.Color = vbBlue

Range("a4").Font.ColorIndex = 10
```

Basic list of colors

Index	Color
1	Black
2	White
3	Red
4	Green
5	Blue
6	Yellow

To find all the color codes (56 colors) you can write the following code, which colors the background of the cells in column A according to the index number of the color:

```
For ColIndex = 1 To 56

 Cells(ColIndex, 1).Interior.ColorIndex = ColIndex

Next
```

- By using the RGB code, for example:

ActiveCell.Interior.Color = RGB(200, 3, 8)

Remove modules

Right click on the module name and select Remove module.

You will be asked if you want to export the module before removing it, for backup use. If you choose to export it, the module will be saved in a ".bas" file.

Using the VBA Editor help

At any stage of the code writing, you can use help in two ways:

1. From the Help menu:

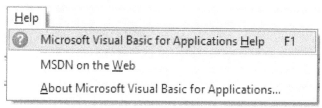

2. By writing a word in the VB editor and pressing F1.

Immediate window

This window enables you to run code lines for examination purposes, without needing to run them from the code itself.

This option is available only while there is no code running (if the code was not activated, or if it reached a breakpoint).

Displaying the variable value

To display the variable value, use the sign '?' (Question mark), and press Enter right after the command.

For example:

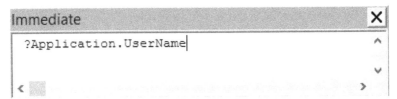

The above command will display the username as previously defined in the software.

In the same way, the following command:

Will show the row number of the active cell.

Performing VBA commands

Type the command (without the question mark):

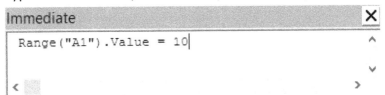

The above command will enter the value 10 into cell A1.

Note:
You can run only one command at a time.

Another option for getting information in a window is by using the command **debug.print** inside the code.

This command does not affect the running of the code itself, and its purpose is to send information to the Immediate window (make sure the window is displayed...).

Keyboard Shortcuts

Keys	Action
F1	Displays the Help window
F2	Displays the Object Browser
F3	Displays the next search result, after closing the Search window
Shift+F3	Displays the last search result, after closing the Search window
F4	Displays the Properties window
F5	Runs the entire procedure
F8	Runs the procedure step-by-step
F9	Adds and removes a breakpoint in the line where the cursor is located
Shift+F8	Step Over - While running a code in a' step-by-step' mode, which calls to another code, this keyboard shortcut enables the external code to be run as a whole, without entering into it
Ctrl+F8	Runs the code to the point where the cursor is
Ctrl+Shift+F8	Stops the code's running

Keys	Action
Ctrl+Shift+F9	Removes all breakpoints
Ctrl+C	Copy
Ctrl+X	Cut
Ctrl+V	Paste
Ctrl+Y	Cut an entire row
Ctrl+E	Displays the export code window
Ctrl+M	Displays the import code window
Ctrl+F	Displays the search window
Ctrl+G	Displays the immediate window
Ctrl+H	Displays the replace window
Ctrl+R	Displays the project explorer window
Ctrl+Z	Cancels the last action
Tab	Indents one line in
Shift+Tab	Indents one line out
Ctrl+Tab	Go to the next module
Ctrl+Break	Stops the code from running (especially effective when the code enters an infinite loop and we want to stop its execution)

Useful Codes

Cancel the copy/cut lineal

After a copy or cut command, the cell remains selected until the following command is executed:

```
Application.CutCopyMode = False
```

Range borders selection

```
Selection.Borders.LineStyle = xlSolid
```

Macro recording which adds borders to a range will result in a long macro, which adds a borderline to each border – upper, lower, right, left, and middle borders (try it...). The above code will make the process shorter.

Sending a file by email

```
ActiveWorkbook.SendMail ("YourName@YourMail.com")
```

Making a "beep" sound

```
Beep
```

Get Excel's User Name

```
MyUser = Application.UserName
```

Get Windows User Name:

```
MyUser = Environ("username")
```

Creating a 'switch' for value changes

Some actions in Microsoft Excel have two possible states, such as freezing a window. You can freeze a window or cancel the freezing. You can write two codes, one for freezing a window, and another one for unfreezing it. However, it is more elegant to write only one code, which checks the current value, and replaces it with the other one.

```
FrzPn = ActiveWindow.FreezePanes
ActiveWindow.FreezePanes = Not FrzPn
```

In the example above, we entered into a variable the command for freezing a window (which can get the value True or False).

Then we used the command NOT in order to change the value from True to False, and vice versa.

You can use this short code for the same action:

```
ActiveWindow.FreezePanes = not(ActiveWindow.FreezePanes)
```

Preventing alerts

```
Application.DisplayAlerts = False
```

Explanation:

Many operations in Microsoft Excel display a message to the user.

For example, closing a workbook without saving the changes will display a dialog box asking whether to save your changes or not.

This code cancels those alerts.

Use it only if you want to prevent the user from having this choice.

You can change the command from False to True during the code, so you can have parts in the code that will not display alerts, and other parts that will.

Exercises

Exercise 1 – macro recording for the conversion of formulas to values

1. Open the file SALES_2007.xls and select the January sheet.
2. Record a new macro (according to your version).
3. Give the macro the name My_Macro and save it in the current workbook.
4. Record the following operations:
   a. Select cell A1.
   b. Select the entire data range (using the shortcut key Ctrl+*).
   c. Copy the entire range.
   d. Don't change the selected cell.
   e. Right click and select the option paste special.
   f. Select the value option.
   g. Press Esc to cancel the copy state.
   h. Press the shortcut key Ctrl+Home to go back to cell A1.
   i. Press the button Stop Recording.
5. Check the recording:
   a. Select the February sheet.
   b. Check columns D and E – do the cells contain formulas?
   c. Press Macros
   d. In the displayed dialog box, select My_Macro and press the Run button.
   e. Check whether the cells in the discount column contain values.

Check whether the macro is working properly on the March sheet as well.

Save the changes in a file. The saving includes the macro you have just recorded.

Exercise 2 – editing an existing macro

1. Open the file SALE_2007.xls.

2. Open the VB editor Visual Basic

3. Select the Edit button.

4. Now you can see the code as it was written while being recorded.

5. Place the cursor before the End Sub line.

6. Add the following code lines:

```
Range("A1").Select

Range(Selection, Selection.End(xlToRight)).Select

Selection.Interior.Color = vbYellow

Selection.Font.Bold = True

Range("A1").Select

Selection.CurrentRegion.Select

Selection.Borders.LineStyle = xlSolid

Range("a1").Select

MsgBox ("Congratulations, you have just written your first code")
```

7. Close the VBA editor and go back to the Excel file.

8. Go to the April sheet.

9. Run the macro My_Macro on the April sheet.

10. Click the message which appears at the end of the running code.

Did your typed additions take place?

Did you get a congratulations message?

If so, you just wrote your first real code!

Exercise 3 – writing code for data ranges
1. Open the file ranges.xls in sheet 1.
2. Open the VBA editor and create a new module.
3. Add a new macro and name it My_Ranges.
4. Write a code that performs the following actions:
   a. Select cell A1.
   b. Select the data set range in column A (from cell A1 to the last cell with data in the column).
   c. Color the range in blue.
   d. Select all cells with data in the range.
   e. Align the cells' content to the center.
   f. Go to the cell below the last data cell in column A.
   g. Add the text "new row".
   h. Go to the next cell in the row (in column B) and color it in yellow.
   i. Go to cell A1.
5. Run the code step by step and check if it works properly on the table in sheet 2 as well.

Exercise 4 – writing a code using 'With' structure
In a new Excel file, write a code that performs the following actions:
1. Select a range that begins with the cell A1, but its size is unknown.
2. On the selected range, we will perform the following actions using 'With' structure:
   a. Centralize the text.
   b. Color the cells in red.

c. Color the text in yellow.

d. Change the font size to 11.

e. Set border lines to the table cells.

f. Enter the value 1234 in each table cell.

Note

The code should work properly for every table range we will run it on.

At the end of the code, cell A1 will remain selected.

Exercise 5 - Loops

In this exercise, you will create the colors board.

Remember, each color in Excel has a numeric value (the number of the color yellow is 6, for example, and we call it by the command colorindex=6).

1. Write the color's numbers (from 1 to 56) in column A.

2. Color the font in each cell in column A by its index number (for example, the font of the cell with the number 6 will be colored in yellow).

3. The adjacent cell in column B will be colored by using the index color number of column A .

Exercise 6 – loops combined in an IF command

1. Write a work plan for checking a range of cells:

a. Cells which contain a positive even number will be colored in yellow.

b. Cells which contain a positive odd number will be colored in blue.

c. Cells which contain a non-integer number will be colored in red.

d. Cells which contain a negative number will be colored in green (even if they were previously colored in a different color).